REUBEN'S HUNT FOR A HOME

Julie Kennedy Fogarty

Illustration by Aaron R.

I0108769

JKF
JULIE KENNEDY FOGARTY
CHILDREN'S AUTHOR

www.juliekennedyfogarty.com

Author: Julie Kennedy Fogarty
Illustrator: Aaron R.

Copyright © 2025 by Julie Kennedy Fogarty. All rights reserved. No part of this publication may be reproduced, stored or transmitted in any form or by any means, electronic, mechanical, photocopying, recording, scanning, or otherwise without written permission from the publisher. It is illegal to copy this book, post it to a website, or distribute it by any other means without permission. This novel is entirely a work of fiction. The names, characters and incidents portrayed in it are the work of the author's imagination. Any resemblance to actual persons, living or dead, events or localities is entirely coincidental.

Published by Julie Kennedy Fogarty. Printer: Amazon. Publisher: JKF Consultancy Ltd.

This book has been designed and manufactured in accordance with the general safety requirement laid down in Article 5, GPSR. ISBN printed on back cover. EU authorized representative: Julie Kennedy Fogarty

To James

ABOUT AUTHOR

Julie is a picture book writer with a passion for crafting stories filled with humor, heart, and unforgettable characters. Several of her books have received recognition in prestigious UK literary competitions.

With a PhD in economics and over 15 years of experience in industry and academia, Julie has made a creative leap into the world of children's literature. Now living in the wild Irish countryside with her husband and young children, she finds endless inspiration in the everyday chaos of family life.

In a lush, green bog where the cattails swayed,
Reuben the frog spent his happiest days.

His home was so peaceful, so cosy, so neat,
With mossy-soft pillows that cushioned his feet.

But the sun grew fierce, and the streams ran dry,

The bog disappeared 'neath a hot, stark sky.

Reuben lost hope, his heart filled with gloom—

His home in the bog had turned to a tomb.

So he tied up his pack
and set off to roam,

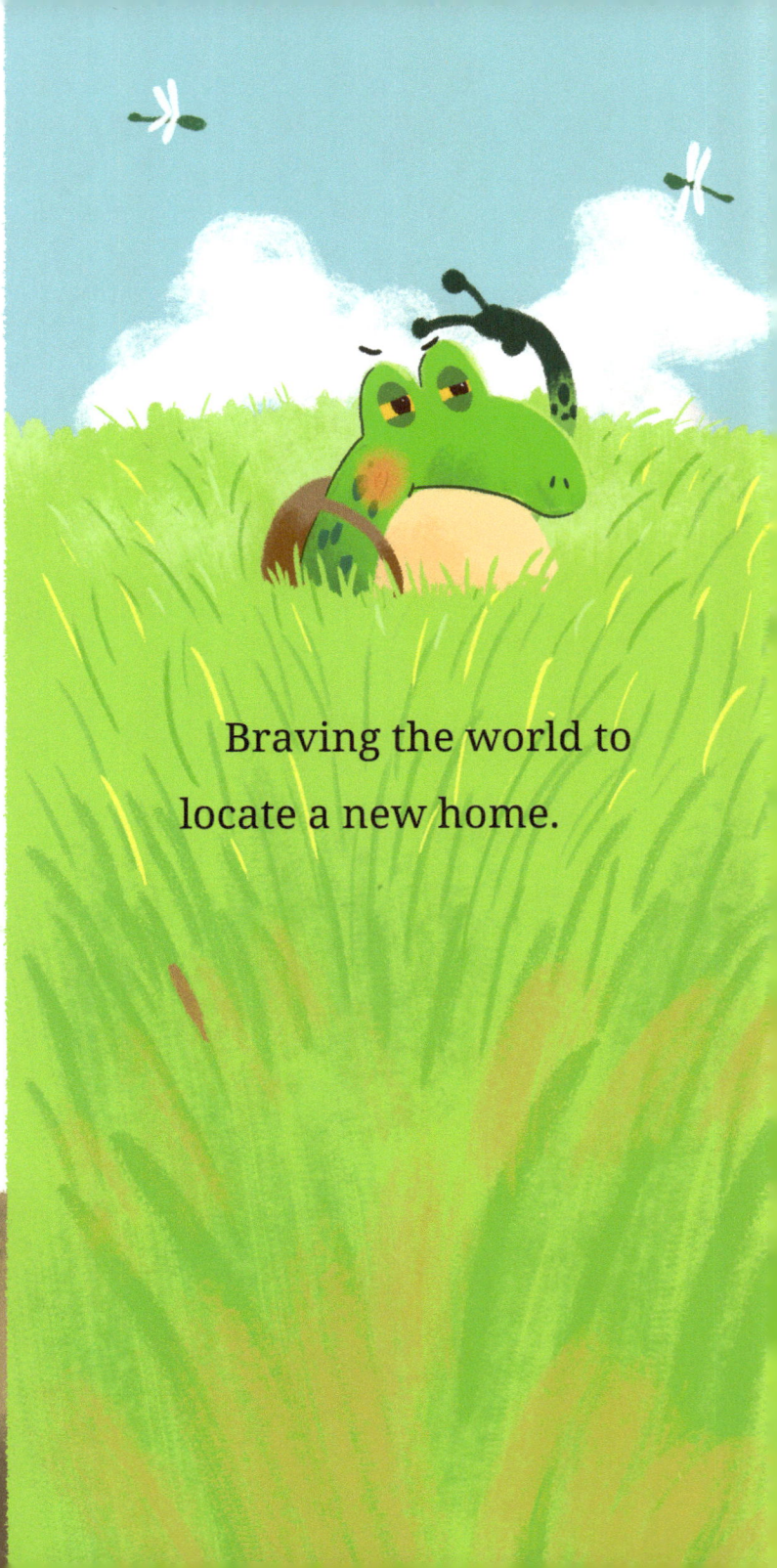

Braving the world to

locate a new home.

Through forests and fields,
he searched far and wide,

Hoping to find
a good place to reside..

By the shore, where the ocean was humming a tune,

Reuben's eyes sparkled beneath the bright moon.

"A rock pool! It's perfect!" he happily cried,

"The sand is so soft, and the pool's deep, and wide."

But within half an hour, he'd fled from its side,

Hurrying off from the fast-rising tide.

He gave it his all and explored different spaces,

Stumbling upon the most curious...

...Places

"Too high, too low,
too misty, too tight,

Too slimy, too bumpy,
too dreary—not right!"

"These places won't work," sighed the sad weary frog.
"Nothing feels perfect—not like my bog."

At dawn, he stretched, he yawned, and pressed on.

He passed by a den, near some rocks, on the lawn.

But as he hopped by, enjoying the air,

A sly, sneaky fox yelped and sprang from his lair!

The fox licked his lips and he gave a sly grin.

"What's the rush? Won't you stay? I'm inviting you in.

There's plenty of space, and it's cosy inside."

"No way!" hollered Reuben and leapt off to hide.

The horizon blushed amber and stars twinkled bright,

As Reuben sat down in the soft evening light

His head was hung low, his heart full of doubt,

When a voice from the darkness abruptly called out:

"Pardon me," coughed a bat, "my name is Jerome.
I'm also in search of a place to call home."

Reuben reflected and scratched at his head.
"I'd welcome a travel companion," he said.

The two scurried off
   through the hush of the night,
   Gliding and hopping by
   soft silver light.

They wandered for hours
   through forests and fields,

Till a fence wrapped in flowers at last was revealed.

They ventured inside and discovered a well—

Although, in the air, was a very strange...

... smell.

Then the two heard a sound that they'd not heard before,

And deep from the well came a frightening roar.

"An ogre I am, and hungry is me,

I need something tasty to eat for my tea."

Up rose the ogre, his eyes burning red.

"I'll start with that bat—he'll make a fine spread!"

"No way!" cried Jerome, as he flapped to the sky,

But he wobbled in fear as he'd climbed up too high!

And down, like a stone,
went Jerome as he fell—
stumbling, tumbling, into the well.

The ogre grabbed Reuben and
held him up high.
"Your little green legs
will be great in a pie!"

And up from the well rose Jerome, with a wail,
Dripping with mud looking horribly pale.

"A ghost!" cried the ogre,

his face filled with dread,

As he stumbled and trembled,

then turned and he fled.

The friends sat together to rest for a while,

Then Jerome looked around and he said with a smile,

"The ogre is gone, and there's no one in sight.

Perhaps we have found us a home that feels right."

The two got to work—cleaning, arranging,

Turning the space into something amazing.

Their home was now ready, all tidy and bright,

When soft steps approached in the dim evening light.

A shadow emerged—their hearts filled with fear.

The ogre stood quietly, shedding a tear.

He held out a basket and gave a small plea,

"Would you fellas be willing to share here with me?"

Jerome and sweet Rueben both nodded with glee—

Their home had now grown from a duo to three!

They set up a table and lit it with cheer,

Preparing a feast as the evening drew near.

"This really is perfect!" said Reuben the frog,

As they laughed, and they ate by the well on a log.

So the ogre, the bat, and the frog in the end,
Discovered that home is best shared with a friend.

Don't miss out on these other exciting adventures:

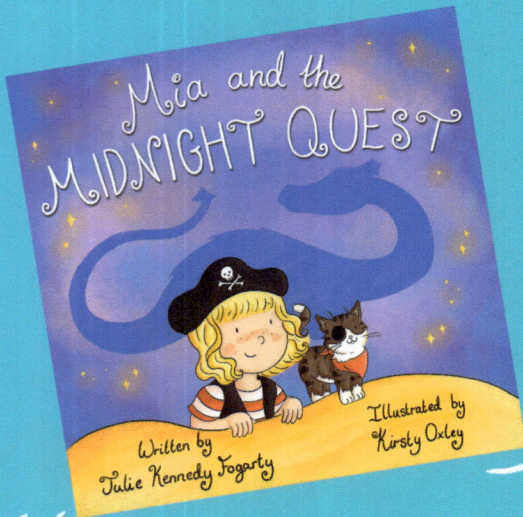

Mia and the MIDNIGHT QUEST
Written by Julie Kennedy Fogarty
Illustrated by Kirsty Oxley

Julie Kennedy Fogarty
Illustrated by Ira Baykovska
THE COOLEST PET

JKF
JULIE KENNEDY FOGARTY
CHILDREN'S AUTHOR

www.juliekennedyfogarty.com

www.ingramcontent.com/pod-product-compliance
Lightning Source LLC
Chambersburg PA
CBHW042056040426

42447CB00003B/246